HORSES

CLYDESDALE HORSES

JANET L. GAMMIE
ABDO & Daughters

Published by Abdo & Daughters, 4940 Viking Drive, Suite 622, Edina, Minnesota 55435.

Library bound edition distributed by Rockbottom Books, Pentagon Tower, P.O. Box 36036, Minneapolis, Minnesota 55435.

Printed in the United States.

Cover Photo credit: Julie Green
Interior Photo credits: Julie Green, pages 5, 7, 9, 11, 15, 17, 19
Heartland Images, page 13
Firth Photobank, page 21

Edited by Bob Italia

Library of Congress Cataloging-in-Publication Data

Gammie, Janet L.
  Clydesdale Horses/ Janet L. Gammie.
    p.   cm. — (Horses)
  Includes bibliographical references (p.24) and index.
    ISBN 1-56239-441-X
  1. Clydesdale horse—Juvenile literature. [1. Clydesdale horse.
  2. Horses.] I. Title. II. Series: Gammie, Janet L. Horses.
  SF293.C65G36 1995
    636.1'5—dc20   95-5447
                                                                CIP
                                                                AC

ABOUT THE AUTHOR

Janet Gammie has worked with thoroughbred race horses for over 10 years. She trained and galloped thoroughbred race horses while working on the racetracks and farms in Louisiana and Arkansas. She is a graduate of Louisiana Tech University's Animal Science program with an equine specialty.

Contents

WHERE CLYDESDALES CAME FROM

Horses are **mammals** just like humans. They are **endothermic**. This means their body heat comes from inside their body. The earliest **ancestor** of the horse lived about 50 million years ago.

There are three different types of horses: hot bloods, cold bloods and warm bloods. These names refer to the horse's birth place and not its body temperature.

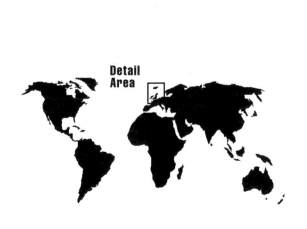

Detail Area

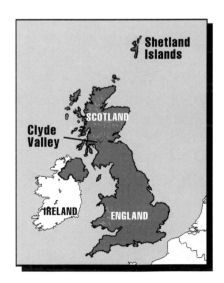

Shetland Islands

SCOTLAND

Clyde Valley

IRELAND

ENGLAND

Clydesdales come from the Clyde Valley in Scotland along the River Clyde.

Clydesdales are cold bloods. Cold bloods come from Northern Europe. Clydesdales come from the Clyde Valley in Scotland along the River Clyde. They are **draft horses**. Draft horses are the heaviest and biggest horses. They are used for pulling.

WHAT CLYDESDALES LOOK LIKE

Clydesdales have a long, lean head. There is usually a large white blaze called a **lantern** that covers their face. On the back of their legs there is long hair called **feathering**. The feathering goes from the ankle to the knee and **hock**. The hock is like a knee joint only on the back legs. Feathering is usually white. Sometimes the white color goes from the legs to the body.

Clydesdales pick their hooves up high off the ground. This high action and feathered legs makes Clydesdales the most elegant **draft horses**.

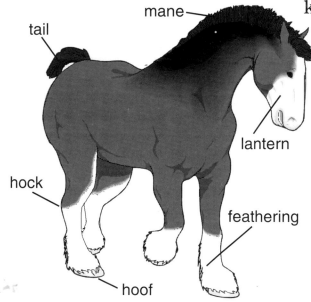

mane

tail

lantern

hock

feathering

hoof

Clydesdales have long, lean heads and long hair on their legs called feathering.

Clydesdales and **shires** are the tallest draft horses. They stand 16 to 18 **hands high** (hh) and weigh 1,600 to 2,200 pounds (725 to 998 kilograms). Each hand equals 4 inches (10 centimeters).

WHAT MAKES CLYDESDALES SPECIAL

Clydesdales are the tallest and lightest of all the **draft horses**. Originally they were **bred** to carry armoured knights into battle. Later they were used as **plow** horses and to haul heavy loads like timber. Today, in some parts of Scotland, they are still used to plow and haul.

American farmers do not like the **feathered** legs and light weight of the Clydesdale. Their legs get weighted down with mud from the fields. They are not as strong as other draft breeds. The Clydesdale has become more of a city horse than a country horse. These graceful animals are better off in parades and shows. Clydesdales make up the famous Budweiser horse team.

Clydesdales are used as plow horses.

COLOR

Clydesdales can be any solid color. Solid colors are bay, chestnut, black, roan, or gray. Bay can be light or dark brown bodies with black points. Points are the leg, mane and tail. A horse with brown hair and the same color or lighter points is a chestnut.

Black horses have all black hairs and can have white **markings**. Roan is one basic color with one or more colors added. Gray horses have white and black hairs on black skin. Gray horses usually turn white with age. Bay is the most popular color.

Markings are solid white color patches on the head and legs. Head markings are star, stripe, snip, blaze and **lantern**. Lantern face markings are the most popular. Leg markings are ankle, sock and stocking. They can have any mix of head and leg markings. Clydesdales used as a team must have the same markings.

Clydesdales can be any solid color. Solid colors are bay, chestnut, black, roan, or grey.

CARE

Horses out to **pasture** need little **grooming**. But stabled horses need grooming daily. Working **draft horses** sweat. The mix of sweat and dirt can cause poor health if left on the horse.

A rubber **currycomb** brings the dirt to the surface. Stiff brushes remove the dirt from the body. Softer brushes are used to polish the **coat**. The horse is then rubbed down with a rub-rag. Rubbing the horse brings out the skin and hair oils. This makes the horse shine. Special care is given to the leg **feathering**. Along with the mane and tail it is combed, removing tangles and dirt.

Vaccinations are given to help stop disease. **Deworming** helps rid the horse of harmful **parasites**.

When grooming the Clydesdale, special attention is paid to the feathering.

FEEDING

Horses need food and water to grow and develop. Hay and grain are the two basic types of feed. Hay can be grass or **alfalfa**. Grains include oats, wheat, barley, and corn.

Horses out to **pasture** need little additional feed. **Pregnant**, working and young horses need extra feed to meet their **nutritional** needs.

Horses are fed three times a day. The horse cannot eat large amounts of food at one time. Too much food will cause sickness. Fresh, clean water should always be given. Horses can live only a few days without water.

Clydesdales out to pasture feed on grass, hay, and alfalfa.

THINGS CLYDESDALES NEED

Clydesdales are driving horses. Their **tack** is called a **harness**. A harness has many parts. The **bridle** that goes over the horse's head is connected to the **reins**. The **yoke** fits around the horse's neck. It acts as a cushion for pulling heavy loads. Straps run from the neck to the tail and around the rear legs.

The horses are connected to the **swing pole**. The swing pole attaches the wagon to the horse pairs.

Because the horses are attached to each other, they act as a team. There can be two to eight **hitches**. The more horses in a team the more weight they can pull.

Clydesdales are driving horses that wear harnesses.

HOW CLYDESDALES GROW

A **foal** lives inside the mare's body for about 11 months. It can see and hear at birth.

Horses can hear better and from greater distances than humans. Their eyesight is also better. They have **monocular** vision when looking to the side. This means they see two different pictures, one from each eye. They also have **binocular** vision when looking forward. This means they see the same picture with both eyes. Their eyes are on the sides of their heads. This allows them to see behind them. Horses also see in color.

All horses grow differently. Some grow slower than others. Because of its size, the Clydesdale, like all **draft horses**, grows slowly.

A foal lives inside the mare's body for about 11 months. When it is born, it can see and hear.

TRAINING

Every horse in a **hitched** team has a different job. The lead horses are at the head of the team. Lead horses are the fastest in the team. The wheel horses are closest to the wagon. They do most of the pulling. They are the strongest. The swing horses are in the middle. Swing horses have a hard job. They have to stay away from the lead and the wheel horses. There can be more than one pair of swing horses.

Size, strength and quickness determine a horse's position in the team. Training depends on whether the horse is a lead, swing or wheel horse. A more skilled horse is teamed with a less skilled horse during training. The new horse soon learns from the old horse.

Clydesdale hitch teams are trained to pull.

GLOSSARY

ALFALFA - A plant with leaves like clover, deep roots, and bluish-purple flowers.

ANCESTOR (AN-ses-tor) - A relative.

BINOCULAR (bye-NOK-yu-ler) - Seeing one picture with both eyes.

BREED - To produce young; also an animal group that looks alike and shares the same type of ancestors.

BRIDLE - The part of a horse's harness that fits over the head, used to guide or control the animal.

COAT - The horses outer covering (hair).

CURRYCOMB - A brush with rows of teeth rather than bristles, made of metal or rubber, for grooming horses.

DEWORMING (de-WURM-ing) - To take away worms.

DRAFT HORSE - A horse used for pulling or hauling.

ENDOTHERMIC (en-do-THUR-mik) - Making body heat from within.

EQUIPMENT (e-KWIP-ment) - A harness.

FEATHERING (FETH-ir-ing) - Long hairs on the horse's leg.

FOAL - A young horse under one year of age.

GROOM - To clean.

HANDS HIGH - A measurement that equals four inches.

HARNESS (HAR-nis) - Equipment used by the horse with which to pull.

HITCHES - A team of horses.

HOCK - The knee-like joint on the horse's back legs.

HOOF - A horse's foot.

LANTERN - A large white patch that covers the horse's face.

MAMMAL (MAM-al) - A warm-blooded animal with a backbone.

MARKINGS - The white color on the head and legs.

MONOCULAR (mo-NOK-yu-ler) - Seeing two different pictures, one with each eye.

NUTRITION (new-TRISH-in) - The use of food for energy.
PARASITE (PAIR-uh-site) - A harmful organism.
PASTURE - A field used for the grazing of cattle, sheep, or other animals.
PLOW - A farm tool used to dig soil to plant crops.
PREGNANT - Carrying a foal inside the body.
REINS - Narrow straps attached to a bit at either side of the horse's mouth and used to control the horse.
SHIRE - Any of a British breed of large, heavy draft horses with heavily feathered legs.
SWING POLE - A pole that attaches the wagon to a team of horses.
TACK - Equipment.
VACCINATION - A shot given to help stop disease.
YOKE - A wooden bar or frame by which two draft animals are joined at the neck to work together.

BIBLIOGRAPHY

Lavine, Sigmund A. and Casey, Brigid. *Wonders of Draft Horses.* Dodd, Mead and Company, New York, 1983.

Millar, Jane. *Birth of a Foal.* J.B. Lippincott Company, New York, 1977.

Patent, Dorothy Hinshaw. *Horses of America.* Holiday House, New York, 1981.

Possell, Elsa. *Horses.* Childrens Press, Chicago, 1961.

Index